I0615348

Samuel Godsmark

Godsmark's Poems

An Experimental Treatise on the Facts and Theories of Life. First Edition

Samuel Godsmark

Godsmark's Poems
An Experimental Treatise on the Facts and Theories of Life. First Edition

ISBN/EAN: 9783744711142

Printed in Europe, USA, Canada, Australia, Japan

Cover: Foto ©Thomas Meinert / pixelio.de

More available books at **www.hansebooks.com**

Godsmark's Poems.

An Experimental Treatise

ON THE

FACTS AND THEORIES

OF

LIFE.

By SAMUEL GODSMARK.

FIRST EDITION.

New York:

RUSSELL BROTHERS, 28, 30, 32 Centre Street.

1871.

PREFACE.

THE AUTHOR *is aware that the literary market is such as might well retard an obscure individual from adding to its superabundant commodities, from the fact that the public taste is so nearly satiated that it is difficult to persuade the generality to peruse, much less purchase a publication ushered into the world under humble auspices, especially when it savors of the "poetical."*

Poetry, although the highest order of literature—in which the grandest, holiest and purest sentiments of human nature are most perfectly mirrored, and every phase and aspect of life delineated in the most entrancing characters—is the most abused. The "Muse" appears to dispense her favors with a profuse hand, so far as quantity is concerned, but quality is essentially lacking, and although an "originality" may be claimed, it mostly consists in decking ancient, well worn sentiments in a different dress. True originalty must emanate directly from the brain and heart, its pictures be drawn from the ever changing scenes of actual experience, and the mind aim at producing something entirely new, and upon subjects immediately occupying the attention of a practical age, and from which something of utility may be deduced.

This I have endeavored to do in this little preliminary work, but as many might ascribe my motive in publishing to a desire for fame, on an egotistic assumption of ability, I may remark that it grew out of adverse circumstances, and that two months ago I had no intention of publishing this or any other BOOK, but yielded to the persuasion of a few personal friends—to whom, together with all who have so readily subscribed to the work, I tender my hearty thanks.

With these few remarks I leave the issue in the hands of my readers. If there be sufficient merit in my humble production to entitle it to a second edition I will greatly enlarge it, and present it in an infinitely superior form in every respect.

SAMUEL GODSMARK.

318 East 49th St., N. Y. }
    January, 1871. }

Life.

—o—

"AND SUCH IS LIFE!" These mournful words, tho' brief,
　Wrung from self-suffering or from others' grief,
　Which greet the careless ear, and pass away
　Swift as electric light; their purport may
Embrace and concentrate the mightiest fact,
With every potent principle intact.
"*And such is Life!*" These simple words convey
That each immortal soul a debt must pay
To destiny—a tribute sternly great—
And bow before the mystic shrine of *Fate*.

　So, ye wayward, wandering child of earth,
Wedded to worldly joys and transient mirth,
Absorbed in aerial dreams or vain desire,
Trim now thy mortal lamp ere it expire;
Then turn its rays, that they may penetrate
And radiate the mystery of thy state—
That Life, in every vacillating view,
May teach thy pond'ring reason something new,
And ope the channels of immortal thought
To trace the hues with which that life is fraught.

　Aye! ponder well, for Life is but a dream,
Tho' mortals all so tangible may deem,

And thus will teach a lesson hard to learn;
Then ope' another page—still hard to turn—
In which experience is there portrayed
To guide an erring soul from whence it strayed,
And bitter truth illusion will destroy
But to refill the cup with truer joy.
While mortal life retains its transient power
We must be scholars to each passing hour,
For every age, tho' but a moment's span,
Receives a destiny ere it began,
And, as we gain in years, expanding views
Progressive elements must e'er infuse,
So, when one problem 's solved and myst'ry 's plain,
Another question takes the stand again.
Thus Life remains a vast prolific book,
At which some men scarce deign to take a look,
Except thro' spectacles of tinted glass,
Or with the reasoning instinct of an ass,
Which will ascribe the wond'rous works of Nature
To less creative power than vests the creature;
Stigmatize an infinite conception,
Its grand design, beginning and completion,
As chance affairs. Because they can't conceive
Its mighty purport, therefore disbelieve;
Because their minds are not omnipotent,
Deem the great mystery as impotent,
And strive to waive the just decrees of Death
By hell-born, fœtid, Atheistic breath.
Without belief, without a consolation
That mortal life is only on probation;
Without a gleam of hope—of power divine—
By which their souls may ponder, and define

Their mission here, their state when Death demands
What good they have to give from empty hands.

Man, the mighty work of God's creation,
Fills the highest place in earthly station;
All living things beside are 'neath his rule,
Because his breast alone embalms a soul;
'Tis he alone whose tongue can warble songs
Of gratitude to Him to whom belongs
The whole expanse of earth. Whose mighty mind
Gave vivid light and life to all mankind,
Inspired his soul with power to thread the maze
Of human life, and rapt'rously to gaze
With solemn awe upon that lumid star
Which sheds immortal lustre from afar,
And pointing hence, thro' mysteries of space,
Bids Reason follow at an humble pace,
And tho' it fail to penetrate the gloom
Which shrouds the hidden pathway from the tomb,
To accept the offerings of his spirit
And ask no more than mortal can inherit.

'Tis true that Life is only shared by man,
And e'en is shorter in its given span
Than many brutes'; but should men thus deduce
That geese and serpents find a holier use
For their poisonous fangs and cackling tongues
In some bright sphere, which after death belongs
To souls of *cats* and monkeys' chatt'ring ghosts,
With all the motly groups of canine hosts.
  "But why," men often ask, "should not it be?
"Can we believe in what *we cannot see?*

" If we have souls, then why should God deny
" To other living things like destiny—
" Make we alone the heirs to joys divine,
" And as immortals us alone design ?"
We answer thus :   That to man was given,
By the Almighty senateship of heaven,
A lease of power o'er all creation's span,
From the first hour his term of life began,
O'er beasts of every name and every grade,
Which for his instruments were solely made:
Whether for sustenance or for employment,
For luxury or moderate enjoyment,
Quadrupeds receive their brief existence
That all human life may have subsistence.
The mind and body need some sustenance,
For death must needs result from abstinence,
And animal and vegetable food,
Dead or alive, is nothing more *than* food.
Devoid of intellect the brute has instinct,
While man has both, and each is quite distinct.
Instinct must teach to live, but knows not why
It has existence, or that it must die,
And nothing but instinctive intuition
Leads an animal to fill its mission.
This earth was formed for man, and animal
And vegetable life destined to fill
A destiny which ends as it commences—
To animate the human frame and senses.

The works of God, so infinitely grand,
Display omnipotence on every hand;

The beauteous earth, bedecked with em'rald fields,
Which, tilled by man, so bountifully yields
A splendid harvest, food for man and beast,
And ev'ry fruit, delicious to the taste,
Where flowers blossom in luxuriant groups—
A fitting emblem of our fleeting hopes,
Shedding a fragrance o'er the gentle breeze
Which rustles sweetly thro' the murm'ring trees,
Wafting the od'rous incense of the earth
As sacrifice to Him who gave it birth.
  Where'er the eye may rest some mighty truth
Is sweet to silvered age or ardent youth:
The towering mounts, capped with eternal snow,
Ne'er melting in the sun's meridian glow,
Whose heights rise upward to the vaulted sky,
Beyond the reach of keenest mortal eye,
Whence rushing cataracts, in foaming rage,
Roar an impassioned song from age to age,
And rivulets and rivers, rippling spread
A silv'ry mirror o'er their earthly bed.

  The noble forests of a thousand years,
Which have outlived the human joys and tears
Of myriads of the mortal lords of earth,
And live to witness still the coming birth
Of millions more, ere time shall breed decay
And all its leafy grandeur fade away, .
Are fitting types of Life. The tender plant,
Succored by Nature's hand, gains each instant
Greater growth and more enduring form
To kiss the sunbeams or withstand the storm.

Then from the sapling to the pond'rous stem,
When spreading branches deck the forest gem,
The proud monarch's glorious charms expand
'Till it in full perfection nobly stand,
And summer's sylvan breezes sweep its boughs
With mystic chaunts, and stirs its calm repose
With those sweet, low whispers Poets love
To deem the spirits' converse from above.
But years roll on, and e'en this mighty tree
Must fade, and bow to Nature's stern decree,
And thus its mission to adorn the earth
Is ended—while a million more have birth,
And still will live, *this* paradise to grace,
'Till God's last fiat shall each trace erase.

These great testimonies of creation
Should silence doubters' gross confabulation
On points of theory which tend to stain
The grandest works divine—but strive in vain.
Some men are fools and others overwise,
Some follow truth and others foster lies.
In some the animal will counteract
What *intellect* demonstrates as a fact,
And, as our future state is not *revealed*,
Ignore a truth because the book is sealed;
When evidence exists on every hand,
Writ by eternal pen, divinely plann'd,
That some great agency created men,
That they might read the transcript *of* that pen,
And thus inscribe upon the tablets of
Their hearts the grand solution deemed *enough ;*

To teach their living souls that after death
Some other life will give immortal breath.

Afflictions cloud the day, and poignant sorrow
Endures to-night, but joy returns to-morrow,
And when the sun of life may hide its beams
For days and years, till all existence seems
A burden, bearing heavily upon
A life which, maybe, is but just begun;
'Tis then we learn to long for other joys
Than those which earthly time so soon destroys,
And the great bitterness of life-long care
Leads to a refuge we can *not* find here—
Where the tired spirit soars t' immortal heights,
And revels in the sweets of heaven's delights;
Where consolation sweetly blends with pain,
And promises a brighter sphere again.
But yet some men will eagerly confute
The argument that man *is not a brute;*
That he who governs all created things,
And bears the sceptre and the crown of kings,
Rules with a moral power this lower world,
Shall be in dark oblivion ever hurled
When death releases his most precious trust
And all of mortal life returns to dust.

But is not that a better view of Life
Which shows the *end* of all its toil and strife?
Why should we live? Why should we suffer here
If we no other mission have to bear?
Why should our minds and intellect aspire,
When Life's ambition 's gained, to soar the higher,

And grand progressive elements contend
How much to earthly greatness each will lend?
If all should prove at last an idle vision,
And God's most mighty works be Death's derision.

Could all the monuments of skill and art,
And every labor of the brain and heart,
Be wrought to grand perfection; were no rules
Laid down to guide with skill the workman's tools
By master geniuses; could peace or war
Imbibe its elements except from *power*—
From mighty intellectual supervision,
From grand conception and as grand decision?
No! Then, if true, these earthly laws must prove
That some command must lead ere man will move;
So, in the infinite counsels held on high,
This hemisphere received its destiny,
And as revolving ages live and die,
From heaven's mount beams an eternal eye,
Noting the features in the life of man
From whence his infant mission first began—
Controlling and directing all events,
The changing seasons, all the elements
Which constitute the sum of life and death,
Cast from heaven or thrust from hell beneath;
And when the sands of time, which swiftly pass,
Shall lay its last deposit in the glass,
The great awakening of the souls of men
Shall consummate this Life's tableau, and then
He who has best fulfilled his mission here
Shall in the presence of his Judge appear—

Receive his just, eternal, great reward,
For having God's omnipotence adored,
While spirits swell in sweet enchanting lays
The vaults of heaven with songs of joy and praise.
Then shall the infinite work, which now is veiled
To every human creature, be revealed,
And all the doubts of Atheists be hurled,
With their immortal souls, in that sad world
Where He has said, in outer darkness dwell
The torturous spirits of eternal hell !

Oh, man ! While yet thy·life has one day left,
Before that fleeting shadow be bereft,
Ponder its truths, and may a power divine
With holy revelation in thee shine—
Ransom thy soul from bonds of reasoning clay,
That it may soar to realms of endless day
In wonder, adoration, love and awe
For Him who made thee, and who made the law
Which guides thy reason, and sustains thy soul,
That thou may rehearse and act the *rôle*
Of Life's vast tragedy, and comprehend
The glory thou shalt gain when all shall end
Then, as the curtain falls, thy gasping breath
Shall witness to the myst'ries after death,
And as the thread of Life be breaking fast
Midway between the future and the past,
As dawning joys of heaven shall greet thine eye
Thy faltering voice its truths shall testify,

And men who witness how a Christian dies
May then renounce all Reason's treach'rous lies,
And ere *their* bodies lie beneath the sod
They yet may learn to live to HONOR GOD.

Marriage.

TO E. S. F.

———o———

HEN GOD reviewed from his eternal throne
The gracious work His mighty hands had done,
The grand conception of omnipotent power
Wro't to perfection in an unborn hour,
The whole expanse of earth, of sea and land
Created, model'd by His master hand,
Each living thing, each unit of creation
Received its mission, with His approbation:
The everlasting hills, whose mighty span
Embraces space no human eye can scan;
The snow-capped mounts, o'erhanging precipice,
The belted rocks and foaming deep abyss,
The running rivers and the murm'ring streams,
Dancing and sparkling in the bright sunbeams;
The em'rald fields, the desert's sandy plain,
Where thousands tread to ne'er return again;
The mighty ocean's vast expansive sweep,
And wondrous myst'ries of an unknown deep;
Each animal and vegetable life,
Its vital element, however brief,

Imbibed existence some wise end to fill,
In conformation with its Maker's will.

Then man was formed, and walked and talked with God
Where holy feet alone had ever trod—
Conversed with infinite eternal might,
Communed with holy spirits day and night
Till his Creator formed the great design
Of woman's mission and of man's decline,
Moulded her beauteous form, then gave her breath,
And made the twain one flesh *in sin and death!*
The serpent's power prevailed—the deed was done,
And thus the scheme of Mortal Life begun.

Humanity increased and nations spread,
And destiny its children blindly led
Thro' all the myst'ries of this transient life,
Its sensual passions and remorseless strife,
The one great moving element of which
Sprung from the deed of earth's first born, to reach
A fruit that God forbid their lips should touch,
Borne by the tree of sin, and plucked as such,
Transformed their transient span of holy life
And wro't the destiny of MAN AND WIFE ;
Revealing God's premeditated will   .
To raise a mighty good from deepest ill,
In blessing that which earned His direst wrath
To fructify the purest joys of earth,
That every moral good should concentrate
In married life, and from it emanate

Each element which sways the universe,
Its highest blessing and its deepest curse.

Thus man and wife fulfil the will of God
And represent the purest type of good,
While men who seek their mission to reject
Their Creator's holiest laws neglect,
And sacrifice the noblest joys of life—
The second paradise of man and wife—
For that which immolates their dearest gift,
And will embitter what few joys are left,
'Till with the keenest pain they'll mourn, too late,
Their self-imposed, unreal, unmarried state.

The obligations may appear immense
When gauged, defined, and rated by expense
But worldly wealth, when deemed a just excuse
For waiving moral right, is rank abuse
Of that which constitutes the greatest treasure,
And is itself the true impartial measure
Of earthly good, the only real foundation
Which rears the grandest work of life's creation ;
Where every moral law must gravitate,
And in its mysteries novitiate,
Ere man can realize the true extent
Of life's real purpose and its vast intent;
Its concentrated source of solid fact,
Where he alone receives its worth intact.
And that which young men fear would confiscate
Their cherished *liberty*, preponderate

In evil influence and in distress,
Would rather tend to foster and caress
The projects they conceive and strive to attain,
But fail because they wrongly seek to gain
An after portion *first*, and fear to test
Joys of connubial bliss at present, lest
Their worldly wealth might prove inadequate
To meet the burdens of the married state.
And, though its tribulations may be great,
Its varied joys will amply compensate,
And new born sorrow gender sweeter joy,
Which nought will badly tarnish, ne'er destroy;
Thus in affliction, wrought from righteous ends,
A more equivalent bliss most sweetly blends,
For 'tis by suffering we truly live,
Know what to take, and have one whit to give,
Which purifies the soul, and will renew
And build the smould'ring fires of life anew.

The exquisite delight which love imparts,
From grandest attributes to minor parts,
The mighty power with which it elevates,
The least conception which it generates,
Should surely claim a trifle more regard
Than as a stumbling block, which may retard
Our efforts to secure what might be found
With greater ease upon *united* ground.
And of the ills which emanate from love
The vast majority, statistics prove,
Arise from ignorance, or a sad abuse
Of that which constitutes its truest use.

Love unrestricted by the power of reason
May please the senses for a passing season,
But as it germinates its rich beauty
Destroys strongest claims on moral duty,
Enchains the true conviction of the mind
In coils which kindred evils closer bind,
'Till love becomes a curse, and wrecks at last
All faith and hope on quicksands of the past.
And *what* a wreck ; what blight, what desolation
Follows that tinted dream of love's creation.

'Tis strange that men, and stranger still, that *women*
Should trifle with the only earthly heaven,
In which life's purest joys are typified
And noblest attributes intensified—
Where sorrow finds its dearest, tend'rest friend,
And richest gifts of human nature blend,
'Till life assumes a garb of glorious hue,
Enhanced and freshened by the sparkling dew
Of early morn, and rendered lovlier still
When even's sunset tints the mantling hill
Of golden clouds which wait its royal descent
And sheds its parting rays on life *well spent.*

Oh ! ye who tamper with the power of love,
Pause ere ye seek its potency to *prove,*
Lest it return upon your guilty head
The coals of living fire your breath has fed.
The heart you once instilled with hope and joy
Then cast aside, a broken, worthless toy,

Whose life you decked with pleasing gilded lies,
Shining as burnished gold before his eyes,
Who claimed the holiest gift from noblest man
But to despoil it, and return again
The power you hold to gender good or ill,
Will claim its vengeance *here*, or worse in hell !

Coquet ! thou poor deluded trivial thing,
Thy senseless trifling might excuse its sting
Did you not transform men to weakest fools,
And use them as the powerless, soulless tools
Of your own pleasure, while you sacrifice
The purest trust of youth to abject vice,
Without an object but to captivate
And gain devotion ; tho' it turn to hate
You heed not its attendant gravities,
Nor that you gender worse depravities,
But soon or late the fate you please to mete
To others will recoil to your own feet.

The power some women wield is absolute;
Her character may be but dissolute,
And virtue be a by-word in her mouth,
And crush the choicest flower of beauteous youth;
Yet, with a lovely, sweet, enchanting face,
And form bedecked with every natural grace,
A silvery voice, a rich mellifluous tongue,
Belying even simplest traits of wrong;
Indeed, a devil in an angel's dress,
Doomed to destroy e'en while she may caress.
She spreads the snare, and few withstand her arts,
But yield the deepest passions of their hearts,

Marriage.

And falling willing dupes to broad design,
Each future pledge of joy and hope resign,
Casting their destiny in callous hands,
Wielding the magic, swift transforming wands
Which changes misjudged bliss to grim despair
Without a passing qualm or single care.

I have no faith in gen'ral "broken hearts,"
Because the salve of time soon heals the parts,
And none but maudlin creatures long retain
A morbid liking for a lingering pain,
When their own folly and infatuation
Wro't all their ruin, loss and desolation.
But happiness will lose its varied charms
When wrecked in fickle woman's twining arms,
And taint the noblest, purest atmosphere
Which otherwise man holds so richly dear;
Will chasten all his life with stern tuition,
Blast his highest aim and best ambition,
And tho' the hand of time may heal the wound,
'Twill ne'er again in life be wholly sound,
For thro' this sad and oft occurring stain
The dream of *man and wife* is rent in twain.
But now we pass from falsity to prove
The glorious influence of genuine love,
And that which constitutes without exception
The truest life, in all its rich perfection.

Dreams of wealth, of fame and noble station,
Glowing pictures, wro't by youth's ambition,
Absorb the mind with pleasant occupation,
But need one impulse to true inculcation

Of happiness. 'Tis love and *union*,
Holy and faithful in reciprocation,
Which lend a gilded charm to ev'ry function,
And blends with hardest toil the richest unction.
When once the beams of love illuminate
The heart of man, the hardest blows of fate
Fall with a softened touch upon a life
Absorbed in one great joy—a future wife;
Then the roughest corners of his nature
And each unprepossessing feature
Are softened, moulded, cleansed and beautified,
To match the perfect model by his side.

The man or woman who has never loved—
And such there are—have never really lived.
By *love* I mean that fierce resistless fire
Which ever opposition fans the higher—
A firm, enduring, soul inspiring power,
Which gathers nobler laurels every hour,
Braves the storms of life, of sin, rejection,
Loves when robbed of all its best perfection;
Still loves when weary years have long since cast
A former substance in a baseless past—
Which wanders back in misty, painful dreams,
Yet as an earnest, mournful present seems,
Still loves when love has lost its *charm* in *death*,
Or worse, destroyed by sin's corrupting breath.
This is the love which gilds our dreary life
And brightens all our cares, our trials and strife,
Replenishes the exhausted powers of mind
'Till in existence new born joys we find—
Sways us with influences sweetly tending
To noble issues, gently, purely blending

The attributes of good with powerful ill,
'Till all that holy stands grows holier still,
And shadows which might shroud our lives in gloom
Are scattered where 'tis fitter they should loom.
But still the joys of lovers end not here,
However all-sufficient they appear;
The bless'd communication of their love
Has yet its choicest excellence to prove.

Parental love ! that deep unfathomed love
Which the recesses of our nature move;
An uncontrollable, ecstatic force,
What mind can fully comprehend its source,
Or tongue describe its great unfailing strength,
Its wond'rous might, its depth, its breadth, its length ?
No human eloquence ; aye, richest lore
Of intellect and passion could no more
Than stand amazed, in steadfast, silent awe—
And viewing, fail to picture what it saw—
For grandest language fails to do its duty
In terms which near express its wond'rous beauty.

A *mother's* love ! oh, ye who have it *prize it*,
For those who judge it lightly or despise it
Will suffer yet the deepest, fell remorse
Which ever typified an actual curse.
The time must come when those soft loving arms
Which reared thy infancy to manhood's charms,
That melting voice, which soothed thy childish fears,
And gaily chased away thy gath'ring tears,

Those sparkling eyes, which watched thee as thou slept,
Or overflowed because her treasure wept,
Who nursed thee in thy sickness, and in health
Rejoiced at each return of Nature's wealth,
Who taught thy prattling tongue to lisp her name,
And joined thy frolics, revelled in each game
Which pleased thy infant mind, and loved each toy
Because it gave her little offspring joy;
Who watched thy budding charms of lovely youth,
And fed its soil with germs of holy truth,
Moulded thy beauteous manhood's opening leaf
With tend'rest care, lest it should gender grief
By turning into channels spread with snares,
Which might bear evil fruit in future years;
And whom, when indiscretion earned thee shame,
Sheltered thy deepest faults and *bore their blame*—
Suffered, wept, rejoiced, and all for *thee*,
As my lost angel mother did for me—
Shall pass away, and "immortality
Be swallowed up of life." Oh! dire fatality,
What sacrifices *now* thou'd fondly make
Could they that lifeless form again awake;
What wealth would give for one sweet chiding word,
Which yet in former years you coldly heard,
And maybe stung her kind solicitude
With cruel anger and with bearing rude.
But no! the time is past, her body's dead,
And all but memory now from earth has fled.

Mother! the last sad glimpse I had of thee
Thy form was bowed with anguished grief for me,

For *I* was leaving home and friends, to dwell
In other lands—and there the curtain fell—
For ne'er again my weeping eyes will fall
On her who was my joy—almost *my all*—
For death has claimed her precious, treasured love,
And nought will e'er again its equal prove.

May God permit, dear reader, you may never
Know what it is to part *like this, forever,*
From her who still remains, I trust, to prove
Her sons and daughters' fondest, tend'rest love.

A *father's* love! what words can tell the joy
Which centres in his dearest girl or boy ?
Gauge the strong, deep, stirring, pure affection—
Heaven's attribute in earth's perfection.
'Tis his great duty to correct and guide,
And make his present joy his future pride;
To chasten with a wise, impartial force,
And purge from evil weeds life's future course—
To watch each yielding gift of budding years,
And nourish or suppress, as best appears.

The man who loves his *wife* must love his child
And foster love in it ; destroy or build
The future happiness of all their lives
According as his love withholds or gives;
That moral truth maintains its proper sphere
Wherever *sentiment* might interfere.
The father—loved in youth, when manhood graces
His offspring's life, and gath'ring age replaces
His raven head with locks of silvery white,
And closing day foreshadows coming night—

Gains holier love in venerable years,
Finds a sweet refuge from his former cares,
And in his children's children reaps great joy
For all the love he lavished on his boy.

Thus parents sip the sweetest draught from joy,
And test the truth of life without alloy,
Which binds the human race in bonds of bliss
And soothes the fiercest passion with a kiss.

May He who wro't this holy institution
Bless its vot'ries with a kind fruition
Of every hope, expressed in humble prayer
To Him who formed the words, so loves to hear.
Then skeptics shall restrain their foolish jeers
At married joys, because its life appears
The noblest lot on earth, and nearest heaven,
With its choicest blessings freely given
To gild our mortal life with purest gold,
And such as ne'er is bartered, bought or sold.

Poverty.

SOME men are prone to envy others' wealth;
   Some envy men's success, some envy health;
   Some envy intellect, some envy power;
   Some envy passing pleasures of an hour.
There's little good or bad on this poor earth
But some seemed doomed to envy from their birth—
Who never seem so pleased as when intent
In plaguing others with their discontent.
Nature has ordained that men must differ,
And some be quite exempt while others suffer;
And if we take our portion with a curse
It only makes the matter ten times worse.
   Folks may growl, complain, and waste their tears,
   'Twill brighten not a day in fifty years;
The only antidote the gods have sent
Is to push along and be content.
What if one be rich, another poor;
They each have some afflictions to endure
Peculiar to their case, and fain would share
A portion of the ills they each must bear.

Stern poverty is Nature's noblest school,
And educates whom wealth might leave a fool;
Where all refractory youths are forced to pen
The lessons which will *make* them useful men;
Give power to act and think, to *work* and make —
A fortune, most, no doubt, would rather take.

Here genius weaves the fabric of a work
In which ten thousand hands may yet embark,
And builds a glorious future in a present
Which to a needy purse may be unpleasant.
Should destitution strive, with threatening frown,
To stint the gift e'en *poverty* has thrown,
Firm manhood rouses all his latent power
And saves his gutted ship from sinking lower;
And, like a vet'ran mariner at the helm,
Altho' before his eyes the gathering film
Of death may oft obscure his forlorn hope,
With raging elements he'll bravely cope,
And guide his storm-tossed bark thro' treach'rous shoals
And thereby save his own and many souls.
We all must serve apprenticeship to life,
Nor sip its sweets, but we resist its strife;
The test is grand, the effort grander still
Which wins a precious prize by hard bought skill.
But ye who shrink from poverty as crime,
Because no need its rugged cliffs to climb,
Who gauge its victims by a pampered rule,
Unfit to test the substance of a fool—
Who pride your manliness upon your wealth,
Whether inheritance or gained by stealth—

Recline on velvet, drink from golden ware,
And eat the dainties epicures prepare,
Yet fear contamination in the touch
Of empty hands, but hands which labor much
To make your glitt'ring hordes—time may reverse,
And in those honest hands may place your purse,
And then you'll learn—it may be learn too late—
To render poverty a kinder fate.
   With riches man can frame a curse, or bless
The store of him who needs his kind caress,
Gain glory, education, highest fame,
And best of all, may earn an honored name ;
May feed the hungry, clothe the shiv'ring form,
Shelter the homeless from the withering storm,
And gild the earth with radiant tints of joy—
All burnished gold, and not a grain alloy—
As oft he nobly does; and thus, poor man,
Be generous in your veto if you can,
For know that were it not that some were *rich*
The bed of many poor might be a ditch.
The wealth you envy, and would idly share,
Yourself can make it if you do and dare;
And tho' an " Aristocrat " you roundly blame,
Would you object, just now, to be the same ?
If others have the gift of wealth and station
Let it excite your laudable ambition.
To gain yourself what now you may denounce,
Because its owners care not to renounce
Their *title* to it ; what you would humbly take
By honest labor you may trebly make.

Some men, when *only* poor, assume they've cast
A hopeful future in a baneful past, .
And as the spectre may be grim and gaunt,
Will read its mission and its name as *"Want;"*
And tho' the two are cold and hard of heart
Their special destiny must lie apart,
But will assimilate if men permit
Their energies to flag, and bodies sit
In weak inaction, and in sorrow mope
Over the remnants of *one* blasted hope.

Want can be resisted by the poor
In many instances, if they endure
The prospect of its terrors without fear,
And force a smile instead of shed a tear.
But these conditions are most often blended,
And will increase a rent that might be mended
If sound material were rightly used
And older rags with dignity refused.
While health and strength are ours what need we more?
Why demoralize because we're poor?
While life retains a spark hope has not fled,
But we must lie as we may make our bed.
The hardest lot may still be softened much
By many a genial if not generous touch,
And sympathy exert a potent power
In the most weary, hopeless, bankrupt hour,
While friendship proves the choicest of its worth
And fructifies a lately barren earth.

The sorrows of the poor indeed are great,
But poverty is not so hard a fate

As those who never felt it may conceive,
And still, perhaps, its evils ne'er relieve;
There's joy in sorrow as there's joy in love,
And joy in taking what 'tis joy to give;
There's joy in hardest toil, in poorest fare;
There's joy in every trouble man may bear;
No suffering, no affliction, loss or pain,
But some sweet gift will fill its place again.

   Tho' wrested from the last of all our gold
Is life less sweet because the tale is told?
The sunbeams still play o'er the glistering dew
Of early morn, which dawns as much for you
As other men ; then gird your loins for *work*,
And tho' the atmosphere be damp and dark
That bright sun's rays will penetrate at last
And all your gloomy visions shall be past,
And God may bless the *means* you once forsook
And give a hundred fold for what He took.

   I know the sweets of great prosperity,
Have felt the weight of deep adversity,
And in them each have learned, tho' may be loth,
Life's grandest work is centered *in them both.*
   Life has many shades, and each complexion
Is food for sober thought and deep reflection,
And every phase has something worth to teach
Which only can be learned by testing each,
And tho' we shrink from what the task reveal,
In after life we may be brought to feel
Its pungent truths, and gain a rich reward
In having that once lost again restored,

Refined and purged from all impurity,
Which counteracts the soul's maturity.

We, as immortal, therefore must prepare
To learn to *die*, by braving what we fear
In case the casket may be bruised and torn
In polishing the gem which is t' adorn
A better life, a holier, happier sphere,
To enter which we needs must *suffer* here,
And gaining this, what greater, nobler gift
Could be desired, when nought on earth is left—
Our race is run ; our destiny is done ;
Our haven gained ?—a bright immortal sun
Shall dry the rivers of our mortal strife
And shine forever o'er a peaceful life.
But *here* no sorrow floods the sufferer's eye,
No blasted hopes in shattered fragments lie,
No deprivations steal the joys of life
And strew our path with thorns of pain and strife ;
But in the hand which deals its bitterness
There nestles some sweet antidote, to bless
And fill the gaps of misery's creation
Thro' which the chill winds of destitution
May rush in woful blasts—so cold, so bleak,
That shelter seems a mockery vain to seek.

By suffering loss ourselves we learn to know
The keenness of a fellow creature's woe,
And thus can heal a wound with tender skill
When otherwise we'd barely have the will.

However we may feel our life a curse
There's many a kindred soul which suffers worse,

And while we have a share, however poor,
Is there no starving brother needs it more?
Then ye who have a crust, tho' poor a fare,
Accept it humbly, accept it with a prayer
That having this a chastening God will bless
Your cruet, that its oil may ne'er be less.

That some have little, some e'en overmuch.
Has ever been, and must remain as such,
For were all mortals rich life's war would end.
For none would lead the attack and none defend.
To *earn* their bread it follows men must *work;*
But who amongst us would not gladly shirk
So stern a duty and laborious task?
We need not answer, much less need we ask.
Our mighty commerce ne'er had spread the seas
Had not a laboring hand first felled the trees
Wherewith to build the ships, and others still
Had planned and fashioned all with craft and skill.
Our stately structures, noble works of art,
Had never pleased the eye or cheered the heart
Had not necessity inspired the soul,
And fabricated when it left a whole.
Were we ne'er sick we should not value health.
Were we not poor, should not *aspire* to wealth;
And lacking thus an earnest aspiration,
Would never feel that glorious inspiration
Which keeps the soul, the body and the mind,
In one intense, unswerving work combined,
Gaining the road to wealth by earning fame,
Which good work most justly will reclaim

The poor man's portion from a stain so foul
That what he lacks in wealth he lacks in *soul.*

Poverty is noble, grand, sublime !
Tho' by misuse it often genders crime.
Some fear its touch and dare not with it cope,
But in its first appearance lose their hope,
And fall a prey to what would be a friend
Did they its mission fully comprehend.
While some are wealthy others must be poor,
But self-respect can close privation's door
And keep it shut; while fortune, slow but sure,
Rewards the strength of him who can *endure ;*
And e'en the poorest may in time be rich
If they but weave the fabric stitch by stitch.
When youth attains to manhood's golden prime
Others must then commence their race with time.
Maturity has won its well earned wealth,
Then let the youth refuse its gain by stealth,
Nor envy him who, once as poor, has fought
And onward marched, as all true soldiers ought,
'Till Fortune's smile replaced her with'ring frown
And showered the gifts with which his path is strewn.
Look upward ! Onward ! Flag not for an hour,
And as you strive forget that you are poor.
The noblest, grandest, stateliest pride of man
Is having nothing when he first began
His contest with the world, and sought the field
With firm determination for his shield,
Resistance for his sword, and trust in God,
That he might find the path where fortune trod.

And tho' we fail, and lose the all we make,
It matters not, there's plenty more to take;
And tho' the sacrifice may rankle sore,
We but resume the place we held before.
Defeat should not discourage—try again;
We shall not find our energy in vain.
Our path may be obscure, our mission humble,
But we may higher rise howe'er we stumble,
And losing much, retaining self-reliance,
Can bid the hard cold world a brave defiance;
For Fortune favors those who boldly seek,
And loves her votaries, however meek.
Howe'er swift she run we may o'ertake her,
And shout triumphantly at last, "*Eureka!*"
And if the hand of fate should interpose
And check the race, 'tis better to oppose
Than weakly grumble at the erratic course,
When forced to travel with an empty purse.

The *truest* pleasure represents the pace
At which we run, and tho' we lose the race
Our happiness will never be the less
'Till we receive the blow or kind caress,
For even if we win the sequel shows
That many a keen, sharp thorn may stud a rose;
And, tho' we wear the laurels on our breast,
We lose the unction when we stay *request ;*
What we receive in cool reality
Is little when compared to ideality;
Then if we rise or fall, no matter which,
The true delight consists in *getting* rich.

Temperance vs. Total Abstinence.

—o—

Some men, born in chronic fomentation,
   Effervesce with much determination,
   As if their bubbling and excited state
   Evidenced a wise and well stocked pate;
Lecture and impart without permission,
Because they please to adorn a mission,
And minister to men their ultra notions
In vapid, crude, and nauseating potions;
Earning more disgust for drug and doctor
Than estimation as a benefactor.

   Fanaticism's soil is most prolific,
Generating a divine specific
For the ills, corruptions and excesses
Which its "advocate" the most distresses,
And 'mid the varied faults at which they rave
There's naught so potent as a "drunkard's grave."
While all true principles of temperance
Are injured by their lack of common sense,
Fevered imagination and *weak* brain,
Which, as an overloaded water main,

Prematurely cracked, explodes in haste,
And all its liquid treasure runs to waste.
　Plumed with the notion that they are inspired
Their wat'ry zeal is indiscreetly fired,
And, once baptized in confraternity,
They plug the outlet to eternity
With condemnations of the wilful soul
Who dares to patronize the "flowing bowl,"
And would have the world make restitution
For fools' crimes and self-caused destitution;
Condemn indulgence, tho' in mod'rate use,
Because its principles some men abuse;
Have Legislative power assist their cause
By framing unjust, arbitrary laws,
Storming freemens' rights, and inclinations,
And sound principles, with wat'ry rations.

　But evil lurks in every form and guise
Which sinful nature's cunning can devise;
With every pleasure and each passing joy
Some element of ill will mostly cloy,
And by insatiate lust and fierce desire
Transform a latent spark to raging fire,
Which, unchecked by reason, soon destroys
Life's truest blessing and most equal poise.
　And *temperance* is that which can resist
An evil, while temptation may persist
In making proselytes of knaves and fools,
Who for a drunken revel stake their souls;
Which reason dictates to discriminate
'Twixt good and ill, nor to appropriate

The gift of Nature with a sottish greed,
Or seek *indulgence* in a simple need.
And, tho' the crime of drunkenness be great,
All *sober* men decline to advocate
The doctrine of an abstinence fanatic,
That sinners to be saints must be *aquatic.*

But some stanch brothers of a *gushing* " League"
Will *spout* for many hours with small fatigue,
And argue, with a glowing eloquence,
That water is of vital consequence
In cleansing morals from an inward rust
And washing spirits from their mortal crust.

" Beware!" cries brother Aqua, " Friends, beware
" Of drunkenness, the mod'rate drinker's snare.
" Wine is a mocker, and strong drink a raging
" Which grows the fiercer while the thirst assuaging ;
" The more men drink the more they will desire,
" 'Till soul and body burn in liquid fire.
" You cannot sip nor touch a sparkling wine,
" Altho' the purest produce of the vine,
" But it will taint your nature, and will doom
" A short existence to a living tomb.
" A drunkard's portion fills that glitt'ring cup,
" Whether you merely taste or drink it up.
" When once you take this step all hope is lost,
" And as the purchase so must be the cost;
" I draw no difference nor demarcation
" Between a luxury or simple ration—
" Between indulgence or a temperate use,
" A mod'rate custom or a rank abuse—

"The man who *drinks* must bear a drunkard's name,
" And in a sot's carousal share the shame."

Thus have I heard these gentlemen denounce
The *crime* of men who care not to renounce
Their right to please a lawful inclination,
Enjoy their wine, and risk denunciation
From lips which frame, from mental indigestion,
A damning answer ere one asks a question.

Such words were cast, with most impressive force,
At my devoted head; nay, even worse,
By one who bathed his principles in water
And styled himself a " temperance supporter;"
Professed that all perfections must adhere
To mortals who condemn a glass of beer,
And that the doctrine first and last imputed
Is that the soul is lost unless *diluted.*
And yet that man is now committing treason
'Gainst each dictate of the merest reason
By advocating anti-temp'rance notions
In unrestrained debauch and deepest potions.
From early youth his principles were trained
To abstinence—and these were well retained,
With credit to himself and to the cause
He weakly deemed the best of moral laws,
Until the influence of actual life
Conquered his prejudices, once so rife,
Subdued his reason by a fierce desire,
Which shattered conscience only fanned the higher.

From which we can deduce that Nature asks
No forced restrictions or unusual tasks,
Offers her richest gifts with lavish hand,
But scorns the fool whose mind cannot withstand
Seductions of excess, and falls a snare
To depths of weakness idiots cannot share.
And should moral strength resign the palm
Which only saves a blinded youth from harm,
Desire and passion, once as strongly caged,
When by temptation's influence enraged,
Will burst their life-bound bonds with reckless haste,
A new intoxicating joy to taste;
And thus his principles will fast decay,
And once invulnerable precepts lay
Broken, blasted, crushed and wrecked, alas!
In what he once denounced, a tippler's glass;
    For Nature, robbed for years of simple right,
When Indiscretion seeks to test her might,
Retaliates with cold, relentless power,
And fetters youth in vice within an hour.
But he who has been taught to moderate
His inclinations, and discriminate
'Twixt legitimate pleasures and the vices
Which throng in paths of life in strange devices,
Knows by tuition and experience
That true knowledge and most strong adherence
To life's best portion is to test the whole,
Nor shun to blend his nature with his soul,
Will not reject a favor and a friend
Because some vicious attributes may blend

To punish those who madly satiate
The wants of Nature at a sottish rate.

True temp'rance I admire; but that the " pledge,"
As enthusiasts glowingly allege,
Is Nature's noblest way to be divine,
And he who *dares* to drink a glass of wine,
Tho' strictly temperate, is ten times worse
Than he who forms and then rejects a *curse*,
I must submit evinces inconsistence
In gauging principles of true resistance,
For he who can withstand a great temptation,
By traversing a line of demarkation
Which assigns the paths of right from wrong,
Proves to possess an intellect more strong,
A sterner reason, nobler moral caste,
Than he who's forced to adopt the course at last,
When good example shows the enormity
Of what is self-imposed infirmity,
But daring not to trust true temperance
Shelters and saves his life in *abstinence*.

A temperate life, in abstinence or slight
Indulgence, is and ever must be right;
But he who dares assert, as many do,
A theory so thoroughly untrue,
That men who love the produce of the vine,
Nay, may at times to jovialty incline,
Pander to evil and support a crime
Too base to picture in this humble rhyme,

Must either lack experience or the strength
Of mind to clip desire to sober length.
  As prejudice must surely clog the mind,
And hardly judge of liberal mankind,
An analysis is worthy small respect
By men who never *test* what they dissect.

  Real temperance men, of principle and sense,
Will shun to annoy and offer deep offence,
By bigoted disgust and reprehension
Of that which meets their lawful condemnation
When made the slaves of *lust* and sinful passion,
Blasting immortal life without compassion.
But *some* who adapt their principles to *gain*,
Inflamed by prejudice, would please arraign
Their brethren who may differ at the bar
Of outraged Nature, and indeed debar
Their precious souls from heavenly fruition
Because they may resent their crude tuition.
'Tis such at whom I take my truest aim: –
Who, if they care, may render me the same.

  Noble temperance men! I gladly hail
Your great determination to assail
An evil which pollutes the atmosphere,
And fills each crevice in this lower spere;
Ne'er cease to raise in eloquence your voice
'Gainst drunkenness, and may your hearts rejoice
In reclamation of a mortal's name
From all the horrors of a drunkard's shame.

Raise high the banner of your righteous cause,
And may each tempted soul obey its laws;
May God support and bless an earnest aim
To save an erring man from even blame;
Then shall the *curse* of wine resign its breath
And fill the grave it dug for moral death.

But they who haunt the cause with spectral dreams,
And bigoted and most obnoxious themes,
Disport their sentiments in Godly guise
When all is prejudice and blinded lies;
Who curse the *matter*, and would save a sin
By emptying wine and pouring water in,
Whose narrow minds, of gross and meanest span,
See evil in the *drink* but none in *man*,
Thus classify the whole as embryo sots,
And helpless slaves to pints, from thence to pots,
And teach that strongest nature can't restrain
A soul from hell until it shall *abstain*,
Are bigoted fanatics, dupes and fools,
And need be soused until their ardor cools.

Nature is bountiful; then use her well,
And pledge her in a glass, but simply full;
Enjoy the blessing our Creator gave
In moderation, and a balance save
For those whom poverty denies a share
Of that which many might a portion spare:
Then shall the wine our Saviour drank and blest,
As of natural bev'rage purely best,
Ere He resigned His glorious mission *here*
And bought immortal joys so richly dear,

Be rescued from its direful imputation
Of luring souls to death and to damnation.
But ye who retail liquors—poisonous drugs—
In shape of bev'rages, shall drink the dregs
Of that with which you succor every crime,
And guileless natures with a demon prime.
Let temperance advocates rehearse their parts,
'Till tempered to assail the hardest hearts.
While Legislative power provides no law
For drunkard *makers* drunkards still will fall
Deeper, yet deeper, in the pits of vice
Which these infernal human fiends devise.

See yonder youth, about to " take a drink;"
He makes it *two*, and totters on the brink
Of that abyss in which he might not sink,
Did he who fed the spark but check the flame,
Instead of quickening the light of shame.
But no !   His cash alone these vampires seek,
Who reckon drunkenness a happy freak
To fill their coffers; and, if e'er his purse
Should fail in that, a thrust and callous curse
Stretches his senseless form upon the stones,
Whereon he ends his life or breaks his bones;
No matter which, no matter *how* he fell,
A drunkard's shame is all the tale to tell.

While this exists let temp'rance lecturers teach—
They'll gender little good by all they preach— ·

And tho' their mission may be quite sincere,
How loud they speak 'twill faintly reach the ear
Of those whom Satan finds an easy prey,
Because our Legislature paves the way.

Sensation Literature.

—o—

How strange it seems that mortals, blest with brains,
Should seek to bind their intellect in chains
Moulded by Satan's hands, and linked with lies,
And coated with a counterfeit disguise
Of ninety-nine per cent. of base alloy
Mixed with a grain of fact, and that a toy,
Pleasing little by its introduction
But rather more by its entire destruction.

To define the *worth* and *curse* of " Fiction "
Test its principles with cogent diction,
Laud its merits, and explain its uses,
Virtues, beauties, and its rank abuses ;
To separate the precious from the vile,
And classify the whole in graphic style,
Which might convince a poor deluded slave
That he abetted in a crime so grave
As robbing nature of its holiest truth,
De spoiling age, denuding early youth

Of all the attributes which constitute
The actual facts of life; and substitute
A false, insidious, visionary cheat,
Beguiling reason to its treacherous feet,
And stamping out what little share of brains
In a poor addled cranium remains;
Wrecking God's best vessel on the strands
Of moral death—must rest in stronger hands
And comprehensive intellects than mine,
Unless the arduous task they should decline.

The " literature " of this progressive age
Keeps pace with people's overwhelming rage
For something more than natural life can give,
To taint the atmosphere in which they live.
Thus, vilest sins, and hideousness of crime
Must be redeemed by traits of the sublime,
And causes and effects *reverse their place*
To admit of being decked with charming grace:
And shrouding fact beneath a false ideal,
That minds may fashion to a type of *real.*
And devilish natures, worse than Nero-ic,
Be rendered pretty, if not heroic.

But, virtues heightened by an ideal leap
To altitudes which make believers weep,
Descended from their bright, exuberant flight,
Present at best a very sorry plight
In human dressing, and in sober truth,
Undecked with glittering lies; and 'venturous youth

Grows morbid in his rash attempts to reach,
In actual life, the dreams that theorists teach,
And in his baseless efforts to aspire,
Sinks yet deeper while he soars the higher.

Fiction which keeps within the bounds of reason,
And counts truth not wholly out of season,
Which neither soars to realms ethereal
Nor tampers with the attributes of hell,
Which dallies with the tender sentiments
Without depositing rank sediments,
Or trifles with affairs of trivial caste,
To be forgotten when the scene is past,
May help to while an idle hour away
And brighten up a gloomy wintry day,
And does no harm, at least, altho' the mind
Might often better occupation find.

Still, as a genuine source of relaxation,
When life's dull cares engender hard taxation,
'Twill prove a good specific, and its use,
While mainly sought to leisurely amuse,
Recuperates the exhausted powers of mind,
And physical and mental evils find
An exquisite relief—refreshing ease—
From that which otherwise might barely please;
And, that truths are well displayed in fiction
I offer no pretence at contradiction.
'Tis sweet, when tired, and weary of the world,
To have the leaves of fancy's dreams unfurled—

To wander 'midst elysian scenes of bliss,
Where flowers bend with wealth of love to kiss
Their blooming mates, and swayed by gentle breeze
Coquette gaily 'neath the whispering trees—
Whose murmur'd songs, in cadence sweet and low,
(Their rustling leaves) in concert hail the bow
Which gives them budding life and beauteous form,
And bears them strongly thro' each threatening storm.

'Tis sweet to spend a contemplative hour
In the recesses of a rustic bower,
Shielded with clustering vines, sweet jessamine,
Roses and honeysuckle, which entwine
Their loving branches, and whose rich perfume
Grows sweeter by each treasure they exhume;
To wander thro' the overhanging grove
And listen to the twittering words of love
With which bright plumaged birds allure their choice
To aid them in their song—in twain rejoice.
To mount sky-kissing hills, and there review
The wond'rous picture which the Almighty drew—
The towering mounts, the gentle sloping dale,
The lovely glen and peaceful sleeping vale,
The winding brooks, and plashing, murm'ring streams,
The emerald sea—whose mighty bosom gleams
And sparkles in the sun's meridian rays—
A cause of gratitude and endless praise
To Him whose lavish hands has fashioned thus
This second paradise, and *all* for *us*.

' Tis sweet to commune with natures good and pure,
And in our views of truth find something truer—
Something we seldom find in natural shape,
Which needs therefore an ideal hand to drape,
That we may feel that rarest virtues shine
In lustrous beauty, and this world entwine;
Which animate the soul to emulate
Such rich perfection—or, at any rate,
To admire an altitude it cannot reach
And learn a lesson that it cannot *teach*.

Did novelists confine their highest pitch
To points where no impediments could hitch
'Twixt earth and heaven, they might etherealize
Their wondrous pictures to the vaulted skies;
But when they seek forbidden heights to scale,
And steal an angel's dress to deck their tale
Of wondrous purity, their ultra zeal
Gains more disgust than love for its ideal,
And men who, fondly loving *virtuous* women,
Despise the pilfered attributes of *heaven;*
For while one dreg remains of human nature
It will contaminate the purest creature,
And those who 're steeled by life to truth and reason
Judge every *natural* fraud as moral treason.
But when these subjects are the novelist's theme,
However overdrawn or stale they seem,
They do not tend to taint and vitiate
Tho' off'ring little worth to appreciate,

And with small patronage—less commendation—
Live and die without much condemnation.

But ye who build "sensation story" fame,
And gain a paltry tho' notorious name
For pand'ring to the worst desires of nature—
Painting sin, and gilding every feature
Which might disgust the inexperienced youth
Who eagerly devours each lie as truth—
Whose "*ghosts*" disport in every shape and guise
Before his vacant mind and glaring eyes ;
"Demons and imps" of worse than hell's invention
Chaining his intellect in wrapt attention,
And deeds of horror, tales of crime and blood—
A demoniacal and sickening brood,
Which float as ghastly phantoms o'er his brain
'Till semi-idiotcy his mind enchain—
Deserve the highest censure; deepest curse
On every cent that swells your well filled purse.

These "writers" waste their most pernicious brains
In robbing others' wits t' increase *their* gains,
Counting no other cost than printer's ink,
And care not tho' a thousand souls may sink
In the abyss of crime from their tuition
So *they* escape the brunt of its fruition.
I knew a "*case,*" and there are many such,
Altho' our Christian friends don't heed them much,
In which a youth of promise early sought
Morbid excitement, where such things are taught

As supernatural stories, tales of "ghosts,"
And awful earthly power of "demon hosts,"
"Thrilling adventures," and the num'rous trash
Which crowd the book stalls in a race for cash.
The more he read the more he wished to read,
And every leisure hour was wont to feed
His fast disordered mind with nervous fire,
Until its lurid gleams could rise no higher,
Then burst their bonds and left him *staring mad!*
In moral darkness, and to reason *dead.*
This is a *fact,* and many daily tread
The same sad track, till life's best gift has fled
To such an extent as surely robs the mind
Of all pure attributes of true mankind.

When *woman* falls a snare to this foul blot
Her reputation is not worth a jot,
And tho' her nature seeks more *sentiment*
Than hideous pictures, still its vile intent
Robs her of all that makes her worth the name
Of wife and mother—turns her pride to shame;
And greatest duties meeting sad neglect,
Her person gains no longer men's respect;
Husband and children, all domestic cares
Are washed away in maudlin, senseless tears,
Shed for a baseless vision, void of good,
And to the purest nature noisome food.

Weak woman's nature craves what man rejects—
Who scorns an ideal life, which she respects—

Because his contact and combat with life
Dispels ethereal dreams thro' actual strife—
Leaves him no time to play with moral fools
And con their vicious texts in Fiction's schools—
Because his mind is formed for *work* and *fact*,
And every passing phase conspires to act
In opposition to the weak attempt
Of visionary minds to coax, and tempt
His reasoning powers to play a second part,
And pander to the weakness of his *heart.*

But woman, much secluded, left at leisure,
Has oft naught to engage her mind but pleasure,
And, if pernicious " books " are in her reach,
She'll sacrifice her mind and time to each
Until its influence becomes narcotic,
And she, wrapt in it, simply idiotic.
That is *weak-minded* souls, who have a share,
Enough of simple brains, but none to spare.
True women I admire and dearly love,
And would not wound their hearts, or seek to move
One glist'ning tear, or earn a just reproach
By one hard utterance, or to approach
Their persons, lives or names, in act or word,
But with respect and tenderest regard—
And such will freely, willingly endorse
This painful picture, if not paint it worse.

I've seen these literary persons sit
Like *statues in an apoplectic fit;*

Their rigid forms would give a sudden start,
Their eyes protrude, their ashen lips would part,
And every feature witness the intense
Delight they felt in losing all their sense.
　Wrapt in the folds of pages "red with gore,"
They shiver, then perspire at every pore,
While ever and anon a sickly laugh
Will follow maudlin tears.　If bold enough
To address them you will find them querulous—
Try to detract them, 'tis but perilous—
They mutter "yes" and "no."　"Oh bother!"　"Don't,"
As if to snap and snarl it was their wont;
And when at last reluctantly they fold
The "paper" thus a *conversation* hold :'
　" How Harry Noodle fell in love with Maud,
" Who loved instead a certain Willie Laud ;
" And Harry, when rejected, fired with evil,
" Swore he'd send poor Willie to the devil;
" So sought him out and cut his wretched throat,
" Then cursed his own poor brains and *blew them out!*
" At which Miss Maud ·fell sick and tried to die,
" But lived instead and married on the sly.
" Her husband proved a drunkard—broke her head,
" Then, in *delirium tremens* put to bed,
" Passed quite a lively time with phantom hosts,
" And bolted off at last with other ghosts. "
And then they make the affecting declaration
How much it did excite their admiration ;
While all around, in slovenly profusion,
Are littered household goods, in blank confusion ;

And they, perhaps the *most* confused, arise
To close in sleep their weary aching eyes,
And blissfully impart to walls and chairs
Their *further* dreams for want of better ears.

Forty per cent. of all the " magazines "
Feed the rising generation in their teens
With food which ne'er digests, but turns to rot,
And makes the cheapest purchase dearly bought.
'Tis true they oft considerately allot
A space to " Household Treasures," " Facts," and dot
The pages here and there with trifling " Essays"
And borrowed jottings—jokes in ancient dresses—
Or touch upon some really truthful theme ;
But this is all the "good" that may redeem
Their character from absolute disgrace
And help to cover stains they can't erase.
And even " Pulpit men " of wide repute—
" Servants of Christ !" make up and follow suit ; .
" *Contribute*" to this cause of anti-truth,
Which mars the happiness of fervent youth.   ·
Thus, those who should be most opposed to evil,
Neglect their Master's work to serve the devil.
Precious wasted hours will ne'er return,
Nor will the useful lessons men might learn
When youth is supple, and whose future joy
Is sacrificed for what ? an ideal toy,
That pleases for an hour ; but, cast aside,
Retains its influence, and will deride,

In time, his efforts to secure a prize
In life's hard lottery, *thro' tinted lies.*
   For once the mind becomes a morbid slave
To baseless notions life becomes a grave,
Where present aerial hopes must sink at last,
A fit memorial to a misused past.

   May he or she who reads these humble lines,
However little merit in them shines,
Ponder well their truth, and if it save
One fellow creature from this moral grave,
My work is done, my recompense is great;
'Tis all I ask; God grant it—*soon or late.*

Religion.

Pure, priceless gem, whose lustre never wanes;
    Source of all earthly joys; whose pow'r enchains
    Our souls in the bonds of love, delight and peace,
    Decking the hardest couch with softest ease;
Whose moral influence can best assuage
The fires of youth, and check the strongest rage
Which leads the soul to spread its wings and soar
To realms where it would fain return no more ;
Where, realizing heaven's abounding love,
Longs when that still small whisper from above
Shall breathe the message from Emmanuel's throne
That Nature to Death's fiat must atone.

Happy the man who, blest with light divine,
The problem of existence can define,
Penetrate the mysteries of his state, .
And link with Providence the law of *fate*;
And, 'mid the principles of mortal life,
Its moral force and fierce internal strife,

Its gloomy sorrows, transient fleeting joys,
Its solid basis and its trivial toys,   .
Has one great object, one great hope to gain—
One bright eternal promise to attain.

This temporary life must fade away,
And all its valued joys must soon decay ;
How soon—how late—the hour will come at last
When earth's long lingering destiny is past,
And God's most noble work must yield its trust
And turn again to earth—its kindred dust.

The noble intellect, the powerful frame,
The splendid talent and the mighty fame,
The kindling eye, the heart's swift beating pulse,
The steady purpose, and the warm impulse;
The love and anger—passion's fitful sway—
The fire of youth, each vivid quickening ray
Which lights the lamp of life, must fade and wane,
And lose its every vestige, but to gain
A nobler casket and a brighter gift—
A substance offered for a dream bereft.

Oh, God! that man, thy handiwork and pride,
Should scorn Religion, and its claims deride;
Reject its counsels, ridicule its worth,
Blind to all attributes except of earth.
A living soul, but *animated clay*,
Without a hope beyond an earthly day;
Who lives for self, for lust, for sensual joys;
Whose wordly dreams all hope of heaven destroys,

When could they feel, for one short dwelling hour,
Religion's sweet, enrapt, inspiring power—
Hold sweet communion with its melting charms,
Rest for one moment in its loving arms—
Sip but one drop of nectar from its fount
Of joy, compassion, mercy—feebly mount
One step to heavenward bliss, they'd barter all
Life's longest span that moment to recall.
Ah ! none can tell the joy Religion gives
But he who loves and in its influence lives.
The cup of life may overrun with gall
But God's most precious mercy sweetens all.
Dejected to despair, distressed with care,
Crushed with affliction, burdened much with fear,
The world's horizon may be dark with clouds,
Which with a gloomy veil all comfort shrouds;
Infirmities may compass flesh and mind,
And grief and sorrow vainly seek to find
Some antidote from earth for earthly pain,
Or in its many evils hope to gain
A listening ear, a sympathetic friend,
Or distant promise of a coming end.
But there the Almighty shows his boundless love,
And sends us stores of comfort from above.
'Tis then our chastened spirits dwell with God,
Recipients of His mercy dealing rod,
And then we feel our need of something more
Than man can offer from his meagre store.

Religion is not learned by worldly good
From costly divans, epicurean food,

Unbridled luxury and pompous wealth
Nor gained by bribery or treacherous stealth;
'Tis no criterion of great estate,
Of education, or a well filled pate,
Nor the essential point in scholarship
Of solid reason, or a temperate lip;
'Tis not *dependent* on morality,
On fleshly feasts nor high hilarity,
On penances, great sacrifice or cheer,
Or reckless daring and excessive fear ;
'Tis not an index from a moral sphere,
To lead its votaries to find it *there*,
Nor yet the pinnacle of earthly fame,
And of a so-called great, immortal name;
One man may soar above ten millions more,
And yet, in God's best wealth, be worse than poor.

All earthly pomp, pride, arrogance and show,
And altitude of power, must meekly bow—
The siren joy of life, its sensuous smile
Masking with luring charms a heart of guile—
All earthly schemes, all sordid, selfish ends,
Bright, airy visions—every hope that tends
To centre life in *self* must suffer loss
Ere man can fitly bear the Saviour's cross;
And then Almighty love, when nought remains
Of earthly bliss, a thousand fold sustains
The fainting heart and sorrow stricken soul,
And makes a shattered part a blessed whole.

Religion.

Religion is a *gift*—the gift of grace—
Offered unfettered to the human race.
God asks no price nor recompense from man
Except that each shall strive the best he can
To keep the casket pure, and best adorn
The spotless gem which His own breast has worn.
That each may see, and seeing may admire
The Christian's badge, and earnestly aspire
To emulate a work whose zeal and power
Grows but the stronger with each fleeting hour ;
That adds a lustre to a worthy name,
To moral worth high eminence and fame,
Beautifies the best of earth's perfection,
Mirrors, heaven's charms in sweet reflection;
Adds a mortal spark to heavenly light,
And proves its moral power *by doing right.*

Good works must ever bear an essential part
Where godliness has graced the human heart ;
But *Christians* seek to emulate their God,
And ask no merit from an earthly good,
Content that none should know or even guess
That they were made an instrument to bless
The weary soul, the wounded, sick and sore,
And aid the needy from their meagre store ;
To cheer and comfort those oppressed with care,
And calm the spirit, faint with boding fear.
His deeds of mercy, generous works untold
And noble nature—best of earthly mould—
May pass unrecognized amid the throng
Of those who tread the paths of right and wrong ;

But registered in heaven each deed is known
Which gains at last a bright immortal crown.
　But still Religion has another *friend*—
A seeming angel, but at heart a fiend—
The hypocrite—the basest, meanest cheat,
Fawns and cringes at its blessed feet,
Because he knows the power it will sustain
With men of worth and reckons well its *gain.*
　With craft enough to see its tendency
To gain respect, and much ascendancy
With men of merit, mind—of course of *wealth*—
Procures its vestures by insidious stealth
To serve perfidious ends and cloak a *lie,*
A fraud—nay, crimes of nature's deepest dye—
With a disguise of saintly purity,
Affecting zeal and lowly piety.
　But e'en *these* people serve a better *end.*
And to Religion's prestige *prove* a friend;
For seeking to disguise their true aspect
Beneath its ample folds, they show respect
For virtues they are forced to don by fraud,
Lest their true intentions show too broad.
These vot'ries to Religion's holy shrine
As valued, useful members ever shine
In churches where the truth of God is made
A servant to the source whence *most is paid*—
Where fleshly teachings puff with paltry pride,
Which devils foster, pamper, tho' deride.

　Should Bishop So-and-so describe a case
Of charity, by which their Christian grace

May be enhanced by further commendation,
They will respond with ample contribution;
Thus gain the world's applause as generous men,
Earn sycophantic praise, and tongue and *pen*
Attest their wond'rous, open-hearted zeal
In *giving* what they'd ten times rather steal,
Should none but God perceive the deprivation,
And *He alone* demand a reparation,
 The baser, meaner crime, the richer unction—
Greater ill inflicted, least compunction—
For while "Religion" can be bought with gold,
And keeps on par *with men by whom 'tis sold*,
They glide to hell with very much distinction,
'Till there their virtues meet with sharp extinction;
And, 'mid the freaks of Nature's crafty skill,
Which patches up the meanest type of ill,
Really the worst disguise of fraud extant
Is Satan's own conception—fulsome *cant.*

 While Truth exists, and Purity sustains
An honored place with men of worth and brains,
These "*creeping things*," of most obnoxious mould,
Which denizen the lowest moral world,
Will missile men with one eternal rant—
Grovelling meekness and infernal cant.
 These "Christians" tell you how "their spirit" yearns
Towards the "dear Saviour;" how their "bosom burns"
With love and adoration for the *Lamb*—
Their "gentle Jesus"—paint the great *I AM*
As meekly ministering to their "precious soul;"
Themselves as spotless vessels, pure and whole.

Watch them at church, and note the *pious* zeal
With which they pray, respond, arise and kneel,
Gazing upon their pastor's genial face
With sanctimonious looks, brimful of grace,
Then nod the head, or wag it to and fro,
To signify to Brother So-and-so
How well *they* understand, how sweetly hear
Mere fleshly words, which make "their case" so clear.
But when the service ends, mark well how strange-
A transformation scene betokens "*change ;*"
They shift and fumble, show a dollar bill,
That all may see the power, so judge the *will ;*
But when the plate is passed the bill is dropped,
And then a ten cent stamp is quickly popped
Amongst a goodly pile of "contribution,"
Which saves the church at least from destitution;
Or, more discreet, they get their full of grace,
Then quietly rise and meekly quit the place,
To save their conscience from a sin so grave
As *buying* what their Master freely gave.
Then, linked with some "dear brother"—sainted friend—
With solemn "Christian" gait they homeward bend,
And in the "spirit" pleasantly commune,
Or as the "spirit moves" so change their tune:
  "Brother, what did you think of that discourse
"Of Dr. Cash? You heard him well, of course;
"I never felt so lifted up before
"And much refreshed; and in that precious hour
"He suited me exactly—made it plain
"That I'm a chosen vessel, void of stain,

"And what few sins I *ever did* commit
" Were pardoned ; that I carried Christ's permit
" To pass me thro' this barren wilderness
"Straight to the promised land; and I confess
"That, as on Saturday I took my rents,
"I helped the blessed cause with—*fifty cents.*"

" But did you notice that young minx, Miss Dash ?
" It is a sin to come to church so ' flash;'
" She never pays for what she buys; I'm sure,
" For tho' she dresses fine she's very poor.
"Her ' pa' is but a clerk, and she, *I hear*,
" A teacher for a paltry sum per year.
" And then to make a show—presuming creature—
" She laid two dollars in the plate. *I hate her !*"
" Quite right," says Brother Snuffle, " very true;
" I always sympathize with such as you.
" And notice Mrs. A., who looks so meek,
" She only paid me half her rent last week;
" She says her child is sick, her work is slack,
" And sundry things conspire to throw her back.
" That I cannot help; and, *beg or borrow,*
" She must pay me down my rent to-morrow.
" She always has enough for charity,
" But there, I think, is great disparity—
" For, if 'tis true it should begin at home,
" She'd better pay her debts. But, brother, come,
" We will not talk of that this Sabbath night;
" 'Tis true they 're in a very sorry plight.
" I thank the Lord He's made me differ much

" In mind, and soul, and worldly goods, from *such,*
" Who must be sinful else they'd not be *poor,*
" And torment Christian people every hour."
  " But still there's Mrs. B., who's always smiling;
" I've heard she's half her time beguiling
" In practicing before her looking-glass—
" Indeed, I see her there whene'er *I* pass—
" And tho' by some she's counted quite a saint,
" Her color must be false—I'm *sure* 'tis paint.
" She don't *look* Christianlike, and what is more,
" She never prays—at least *I never saw her.*"
  " On Sunday last I heard old Parson Plain—
" A dreadful man—I will not go again.
" He was *impious,* spoke of *hell* and *damn,*
" And said *our* principles were all a sham;
" That we were sinners, vile, unclean and base,
" Instead of Christian people, saved by grace;
" Said that long prayers were hateful in the eyes
" Of Him who judges wholesome truth from lies,
" And public piety was oft a *guise*
" Concealing evil deeds with canting lies,
" And other awful things I dare not mention
" Lest you believe I have some bad intention.
" But now we're home, *dear* friend, pray just step in
" And take, as usual, a glass of gin."

So now—*three spirits* join in blissful talk—
We'll deem it *prudent* to resume our walk,
And ask no pardon for our sketch; in fact
It should be more severe to be intact,

These frauds on every precept good and pure
Grow ten times worse ere they become mature;
Thus "grow in grace" till God's eternal fiat
Bids their prating be for ever quiet.

True piety shines *best* in Christian women—
Fit emblems of the purity of heaven.
A lowly spirit, meekness of the dove;
A grand devotion, rich in faith and love;
A blessed charity and feeling heart,
In generous sympathy, all bear a part
(A pungent antidote to earthly ill)
In making lovely woman lovelier still.
This child of God devotes each precious hour
As ministering angel to the sickly poor,
To cheer the hopeless, succor the distressed,
Ease the suffering and relieve the oppressed.
The noblest laurels ever won and worn
Are thine, dear friend, to heighten and adorn
A life of love—to which no earthly crown
Could add one lustre, glory or renown.
The noblest song that poet ever sung,
Or struck from sweetest lyre e'er yet strung,
Fails to record thy virtues, love and worth,
Which shed their radiance o'er this sinful earth;
But if an humble instrument like me
Presumes to add one tribute more to thee,
May God permit it may serve some good end,
If but the brief response of *one* dear friend.

Practical Men.

—o—

Now this universe teems with "Practical Men,"
Who scorn the theorist's soul inspired pen;
Who laugh at the glowing and eloquent fire
Which burns in his bosom, and know no desire
But to study *themselves* and their own selfish ends;
Whose climax of happiness *solely* depends
On a snug little balance from "profit and loss"
And other small treasures of practical *dross*.
Puffed up with importance inflated conceit,
With dull plodding mind and lead laden feet,
A stern cut face and an adamant heart,
With these "Practical Men" must each bear a part.
Thus the plea of the poor but closes his purse
With a snap and a snarl—it may be a curse.
  "Take example, my friend, be a Practical Man;
"I give my *advice*—get the rest as you can.
"My purse is well filled, my health is robust,
"My mind is contented, my dealings are just;

Practical Men.

"I need no assistance, and ask no respect,
"The world is welcome to give and reject;
"I work to make money, and make it I can,
"And keep it as well—like a Practical Man.
"Do you the same; if you don't 'tis your fault—
"You are but a nuisance, unworthy your salt."

Thus talks our *would be* fine practical brother,
Whose sympathy 's dead to the woes of another;
Who looks with contempt on a poor stricken wretch
On the verge of starvation, to coolly fetch
A grunt of disgust, that Nature should give
So useless an object permission to live.
Wrapped up in himself, he cares not a straw
For aught in creation save lucre and law.

The youth's aspirations, his castles in air,
His visions of life, unsullied and fair,
His bright happy dreams and worshipped ideal,
Which coming events might junction with real;
His generous impulse to do and to dare,
To banish all features of sorrow and care,
With his soul beaming over with beautiful trust
In the faith of mankind—the reward of the just—
Nay, freighted with all that makes life worth the gift,
Will anon of existence be grimly bereft,
Should these *practical* fellows receive but a chance
To pierce his warm heart with their withering lance.
For the glories of *science* and beauties of art,
Which to men of true nature are joys of the heart,

For sweets of Religion—exaltation of prayer
And holy communion—they have not a care,
But are merely a *fraud* on life's meanest span,
And *pilfer* the title of " Practical Man"
To garnish their sins with a false shallow gold
That naught will refine, be they ever so old.

There is lowness in Virtue and meekness in Power,
And Genius shelters in Modesty's bower.
The rich may be humble, the wise be content
To ask no reward for great energies spent.
Aye, a man with the cardinal virtues all told
In the midst of life's blessings may stand in the cold.
But men of small calibre—meanness of mind—
To the best part of Nature remorselessly blind,
Who have nothing to offer, much less to give
In return for the gift of their Maker, to live
Know no higher mission than centres in self,
Which opens the portals of bargain and pelf—
Esteem themselves solely as models of worth,
And chief in the rank of the homage of earth.

But *true* Practical Men, whose contest with life
Has steeled them to reason—whose veteran strife
Has rendered them lessons of practical truth,
Which can temper and chasten irrational youth ;
Who will wisely provide for a dull " rainy day "
And still sip the pleasures of life while they may;
Systematic in action, in judgment correct,
Sober in reason and prone to reflect,
Nobly deserve that each tongue and each pen
Shall yield them full honors *as* " Practical Men,"

Fashion's Vagaries;

OR, SHORT *vs.* LONG DRESSES.

—o—

THE vagaries of Fashion are enough, beyond all
    question,
To spoil the mildest temper and ruin the diges-
    tion.
Some ladies are persistent in refusing to admit
Much claim to common sense—*men's* judgment not a
    whit.
I could tell a lengthy story, but prefer to cut it *short*—
" As you would prefer our dresses," the ladies may retort.
Well—yes—*perhaps* I would, tho' dare not say the *word*
But relate a conversation I lately overheard.

Two Broadway belles collided—one short, the other
    tall—
Dressed in the latest fashions, and *a-la*-waterfall.
After mutual addresses, and usual caresses,
Their regards were quickly turned from their faces to
    their dresses.

4

"My dear," said Lady Short, "your dress seems out of
    fashion,"

"If you have not read the styles I tender my com-
    passion,

"Half a yard or more is added to the dresses once *de
    trop*,

"And you see *I* follow Fashion, for Fashion should be
    law."

Said Lady Tall, with kindling eye, "I need no information,

"I equal you in knowledge as I equal you in station;

"I wear my dresses short for the *short* and simple
    reason

"That they are more elegant, and adapted to the season.

"Whenever Fashion *nonsense* quotes, tho' other ladies
    bear it,

"I need not aid its efforts, and I surely will not *wear it.*

"My dress is not a scavenger, to sweep a dirty street,

"To impede me in my motions and—ahem ! *to hide my
    feet ;*

"And another reason is—well, perhaps you may infer it—

"We always have acknowledged that the gentlemen
    prefer it."

Miss Short had listened patiently, but with a gathering
    frown,

And with a *rising* effort to keep her temper *down*

Said she, "You may be right in a part of your defence,

"But I deprecate your hint that I lack in common
    sense.

"The season, I admit, is advancing—*so am I*—

"And am following Church fashion, which is not quite
    so *high.*

"Long dresses are more modest and more graceful, all
   admit,
"And are warmer far in winter *than the wind about the
   feet.*
"Tho' gentlemen prefer, to criticise our gaiters,
"If Fashion should forbid they may chafe until they
   hate us.
"As to sweeping on the roads—Fashion does but aid
   the law,
"And shames our ill contractors, *who never sweep at all.*
"But then such talk is nonsense—*I* can avoid the dirt,
"And injure not a thread—by holding up my skirt.
"Your arguments are fair; but, in fact, they lack in
   strength
"What your notions want in style and your garments
   lack in length."
"I perceive," replied the other, "that 'tis useless to
   prolong
"The subject any further—but truly you are wrong.
"Some, tho' they *are* convinced, if convinced against
   their will,
"Pleased with their own opinion they will retain it
   still.
"Fashion is no guide when judgment is rejected,
"Common sense ignored, and sound advice rejected,
"Ere long you will discover that your care to hide
   two feet
"Will end in dragging *six* along the crowded street,
"And when you find *another* tear the *whole* from off
   your back,
"You may regret the *step* which followed such a track.

" I study others' comfort and still secure my own;

" While *you*, who study Fashion, stand selfishly alone

" Long dresses may be graceful, but in walking I desire

" My hands and feet at liberty ; nor do I much admire

" To see a *lady* occupy the path for full three yards,

" While gentlemen detest the style which business
        haste retards;

" If Fashion runs in Folly's wake and *you* add to its
        train,

" I disregard its weak attempt to steal away *my* brain."

Help Yourselves.

—o—

GOD helps those who help themselves,
　Who brace the nerves for work,
And face the world with firm resolves—
　They will no duty shirk—
Who, having faith in Providence,
　Still in themselves have trust,
And scorn to gain by mean pretence,
　Or eat a beggar's crust.

II.

The course of life is strewn with thorns,
　But flowers sweetly blend,
And many a resting place adorns
　It ere we reach the end.
And tho' we meet with powerful foes,
　Who intercept our pace,
We shall recline in calm repose
　If we but win the race.

III.

The time is short, 'twill soon be o'er,
　And life's warfare shall cease;
Then he who suffered values more
　The boon of perfect peace,
The pass of life is " Go ahead !"
　Work with untiring zeal,
For all must lie upon the bed
　They make—of woe or weal.

IV.

Some men presume that God has cast
　Their destiny in moulds
Which break with every furnace blast,
　And wreck the life it holds,
So fold their hands with meek resolve
　Their portion to endure,
And thus with blind reliance solve
　The mystery *why they're poor*.

V.

Each mortal lives himself to *make*,
　And not to wholly trust
On miracles, that he may take
　What others leave to rust;
To boldly face the foes of life,
　And manfully appease
Its war of sorrow, care and strife,
　'Till fighting brings him peace.

VI.

The world is cold, and stern, and hard
　To those who shrink with fear
From boldly seeking the reward
　Which vet'ran soldiers share;
And heaven pities not the man
　Who fears his fellow's eye,
And that to do the best he can
　He thinks is but to *die*.

VII.

Our Infinite Creator's hands
　Formed the vast universe,
And every element withstands
　An idler with a curse.
The great ordeal of life is *work*,
　Of stern laborious cast,
And woe to him who cares to lurk
　In corners of the *past*.

VIII.

For man was born to live and learn,
　And mould each passing hour,
That for each thorn it shall return
　An everlasting flower;
And he who does reject the task
　Will e'er in gloom repine,
That life is but a hideous mask
　Which he cannot define.

IX.

God marked *our* course and formed the mind,
And every feature noted,
   That to some duty to mankind
Each portion be devoted,
   To firmly crush each bulwark placed
To intercept our mission,
   And not believe that it is based
Upon the world's permission.

X.

Altho' our souls *we* cannot save,
   Or realize our state,
When death shall lay us in the grave
   And close the book of fate,
We still can work with ardent zeal
   To till the joys of earth,
And boldly stand while others kneel
   And plead their lack of *worth.*

Faith.

—o—

Tне heart may grow weary of lessons of woe,
  And the body may quail at each chastening blow,
  But courage ! dear friend, tho' sick unto death,
  Ne'er cease to remember the *lesson of Faith*— .
    That glorious boon,
    Which later or soon
Will infuse us with immortal breath.

II.

Have faith in thyself, have faith in thy God ;
Have faith in His love and His chastening rod;
Have faith in thy mission; have faith in thy life;
Have faith in its joys; still have faith in its grief.
    The tale is soon told;
    Youth soon must be old,
And bid a farewell to its strife.

III.

When the terrors of doubt thy soul may suspend,
And ye anger with fear that new evils forefend—

4*

When thy portion is bitter, thy joys have collapsed,
'Tis but for a period, which, when elapsed,
  The hands which oppress
  The life with distress
Shall yet be entirely unclasped.

IV.

Let Hope, its sweet sister, unite thee with Faith,
That the sharp crown of thorns may give place to a
            [wreath,
And the sun of *mortality* still ever shine
  With a beautiful promise
  Of joy and surprise
In the riches which yet will be thine.

V.

When the storms of adversity scatter thy hopes,
And fair fickle Fortune with promise elopes,
And the seeds of affliction take root in her place,
It is not dishonor—it is not disgrace;
  Have faith in the end
  That flowers will blend,
And all its rank herbage replace.

VI.

But Faith without *works* is a fragile belief,
And its fragile conceptions will e'er come to grief.
To have faith in a purpose, but use not the means
By which earthly substance shall gender from dreams

Is an idle pastime—
Nay, a grave moral crime,
But an error which ne'ertheless teems.

VII.

To have faith in the blessings of God we must *work*,
Lest the gales of theory shatter our bark.
With Hope as our anchor, and Faith as our cross,
Let us e'er steer our course thro' danger and loss,
    And buffet the billows,
    Not use them as pillows
To lay our broad shoulders across.

VIII.

And when dangers thicken, and darkness surround,
Obscuring the haven for which we are bound,
Let Faith never wane, and labor ne'er cease,
And the end shall be rich with the harvest of peace;
    Then God will sure bless
    With a holy caress—
That chaos of ills will appease.

IX.

When death shall at last claim thy shadow of life,
And bring to thy spirit immortal relief,
Precious Faith will sustain thee, and nobly will bear
Thy glad ransomed soul to that paradise where
    Sweet angels await,
    At the heavenly gate,
With the pure golden crown thou shalt wear.

Hope.

—o—

 EE yon guiding star in the sombre horizon,
Shedding silvery light o'er the gloom of a prison,
Where mortals lie bound in the fetters of sin—
Where sorrow and grief seem forever shut in—
How sweetly it beams,
How radiant gleams,
With a glow that is ne'er on the wane.

II.

Whence is it, poor pris'ner, and what is its name?
And why should it lure thee from sorrow and shame?
Guide thy faltering steps to a haven of rest,
When the sun's last beams touch the brow of the West—
When glory of light
Weds the gloom of the night,
And thy soul is so sorely oppressed?

III.

Watch its lingering touch on that poor weary head,
Bowed with sickness and care on a pain stricken bed,

With a halo of glory refulgently bright,
Transforming affliction to joy and delight—
    A luminous shower
    Of enduring power,
Of glorious prismatic light.

IV.

Watch yon golden haired mother, in sickening fear,
Whom Fate cruelly holds 'tween a smile and a tear;
Whose darling first born, in its infancy's charms,
Lies fading, near dying, in love twining arms;
    What glorious vision .
    ·Invokes a revision
Of death, and her agony calms?

V.

'Tis a sweet, soothing message from spirits on high,
That her loved treasure will surely not die—
Bourne sweetly and swift on that eloquent ray
Which the hand of Despair tries so vainly to stay—
    'Tis that glimmering star,
    Which sheds from afar
The bright budding promise of day.

VI.

When compassed around with legions of woe,
And wearily seeking to weaken the foe—
When storms of affliction and sorrow assail,

And our energy flags, and our strength seems to fail,
  Inspiringly bright
  That sweet satellite
Will guide us from valley to dale.

    VII.

That radiant star in the glimmering east
Is the spirit of Hope that our trouble has ceased—
Whose sweet dwelling presence new visions impart,
And faith in whose promise brings joy to the heart.
  Then ever hope on,
  'Till the glorious sun
Of fruition shall bid us to part.

Charity.

—o—

RIM poverty stalks, on misery bent,
  On cruel desolation and sorrow intent—
  The home it visits grows sadder in gloom,
  And shadows fall thick o'er each cheerless room,
    So hopeless and dreary,
    Its inmates grow weary
Of life o'er which sorrows e'er loom.

II.

Sickness is busy, starvation is rife,
And death is contending, to hasten the strife.
Nature is cheerless—all hope has expired—
The last gleam of joy has coldly retired,
    And each head is bowed low
    In communion of woe,
And spectres grow hidous and weird,

III.

But now o'er the hearth sweet Charity's ray
Beams sweetly from heaven, so cheering and gay

That sunken eyes beam and cold hearts grow warm,
And a genial glow floods the cowering form
    Which hopefully waits,
    As a whisper abates,
The parting refrain of the storm.

IV.

Sin has dismantled the beauties of youth,
And evil weeds choked the blossoms of truth;
A tempter has crushed the virgin's birthright,
And the fair head is hid from Purity's sight;
    What bitters she reaps,
    Poor child! How she weeps
Thro' days and the long weary nights.

V.

But the world is cold—her sisters are pure;
No evil has tempted their strength to endure.
With lips curled in scorn, and heads turned away,
With close gathered skirts they pass on their way;
    Strong men and fair maidens,
    Who happiness gladdens,
Leave the fallen to weep and to pray.

VI.

But a hand outstretched draws a beautiful veil
O'er the grief bowed form, so lovely tho' frail,
And with gentle caress o'er the bright golden hair
Bids the fair one abandon grief and despair,

And in Charity's arms
Her agony calms,
And a smile replaces a tear.

VII.

CHARITY! Lovely, refined and sublime,
Thy presence can conquer the essence of crime,
And mis-led youths find a chastening guide
To sweetly save them from life's downward tide.
May thy spirit e'er beam,
As a beautiful dream,
O'er bulwarks of hardness and pride.

VIII.

Oh! ye of the world, secure from its harm,
When others are tempted refuse not the balm
Which shall heal their wounds and cover their sin,
That each fallen sister and brother begin
To live life anew,
And each blessing renew,
That joy be forever let in.

The Soldier of Life.

—o—

Hear the martial note of the bugle proclaim
That the soldier of valor, of honor and fame,
Must gird up his loins for the battle of life,
And boldly encounter its carnage and strife,
    Undaunted and brave,
    In the face of the grave,
To echo the shout of his chief.

II.

" Onward !" still " Onward !" to do and to dare—
Its trophies and dangers to win and to share;
With thy motto emblazoned, thy banner unfurled,
Storm the ramparts and forts of the hard callous world,
    And each enemy cast
    In the grave of the past,
Where armies are already hurled.

III.

Tho' thy fellows their wounds and defeats may bewail,
Still the world's moral forces with vigor assail;

Let thy courage wax warm as the battle grows fierce;
Tho' the lance of the foe thy bosom may pierce
  Still gallantly on
  Till the victory's won,
Nor flee at the sound of *reverse.*

IV.

Thy Captain has bid thee to fight and endure,
And suffer affliction, that life may be pure;
That thy mind and thy soul shall be grandly refined,
While all would be worthless by lagging behind.
  Then onward forever,
  Till futurity sever
The bonds which mortality bind.

V.

Tho' thy heart may grow faint at each word of com-
  mand,
By the standard of Hope ever valiantly stand,
Till thy God shall reward thee with blessings of peace,
And thy labors and warfare forever shall cease,
  And bright realms of bliss
  Greet thy soul with a kiss,
And give thee eternal release.

Home, Sweet Home.

———o———

Long years have passed since childhood's home
shadowed an ideal life,
And shed a halo 'round a head now bent with
toil and strife;
But thoughts will come of those sweet days when sor-
row was unknown,
And parents' fostering love enshrined a heart now sad
and lone.

> Home! Home! Sweet, sweet Home!
> 'Tis vain to seek, the wide world through,
> twin joys of childhood's home.

II.

Wanderers in this wilderness—face to the cold, hard
world—
Our motto, tho', "*Excelsior,*" our banner, tho', un-
furled.

Amidst its triumphs, joys and griefs, wherever we may
   roam,
No love so pure, no thought so sweet, as that of child-
   hood's home.
        Home! Home! Sweet, sweet Home!
        'Tis vain to seek, the wide world through,
          twin joys of childhood's home.

III.

The choicest gifts maturity can lavishly bestow
Can never rend our memory from dear friends, who, now
   laid low,
Once ministered life's holiest charms, which shed its
   hallowed rays
Upon the happiest dream of life—Our childhood's home
   and days.
        Home! Home! Sweet, sweet Home!
        'Tis vain to seek, the wide world through,
          twin joys of childhood's home.

Lacrosse.

TO JOHN HORN, JR., PRES'T KNICKERBOCKER LACROSSE CLUB.

——o——

Ox the field of Lacrosse, on the field of Lacrosse,
  See opponents in battle array;
Both honor and name, and glory and fame,
  Will 'pend on the issue to-day.
Let the standard wave o'er champions brave,
  And each by his motto swear—
Wage a gallant fight, with an arm of might,
  Then onward—to do and to dare.

Watch the ball in its flight, like a spirit of light,
  Speed up from a glorious throw,
On its mission sent, and to conquer intent,
  It answers a ready echo
To the cheers of its friends, as its promise forefends
  The gain of the laurels of play,
And in its repose both brothers and foes
  Clasp hands on the fate of the day.

The struggle is great, and the powers of Fate
  May waver at Victory's door,
And, turning aside, will coolly deride
  The best cherished hopes of an hour.
Then the echoes rebound, and the heavens resound
  With the shout that the battle is won;
But the fallen in Lacrosse bear slightly the loss,
  For the laurel of all is " *Well done.*"

Memento Mori.

THE "LITTLE CHURCH 'ROUND THE CORNER."

—o—

Superstition darkens still this most enlightened age,
And bigotry stalks rampant with anti-pious rage,
Denouncing and reviling, with sanctimonious ire,
The liberal relations which all true men admire.
Now some denominations of a much divided "Church"
Assume their diff'ring brothers will be left in the lurch
When God shall call the muster roll of sinners and of
    saints, .
And of its future destiny each anxious soul acquaints.
But however bigotry may roar, and howe'er fierce its
    breath,
Charity should close its mouth when life has *closed in
    death;*
And, howe'er prejudice may reign, *true* godliness should
    dwell
Where godliness has been "ordained" to save a soul
    from hell.

GEORGE HOLLAND lived, in men's esteem, in purity and
　　truth,
And not a slur has crossed his fame from well known
　　early youth;
Beloved by all who knew the *man*, admired by all who
　　hung
Delightedly upon the power and pathos of his tongue.
A man of sterling moral cast, of ample frame of mind,
And every attribute of truth and nobleness of combined,
When death dismissed his spirit from this temporary
　　stage
A " Clergyman" refused to ope' the burial service page;
Refused the poor, cold, lifeless clay a Christian's last
　　farewell,
And, as an "ACTOR'S " portion, doomed his noble soul to
　　hell !
　　The sorrowing friends protested, the anguished mourn-
　　　ers wept;
But the " Man of God" was callous, and the sad pro-
　　cession left;
Then a " Little Church 'Round the Corner "—an humble
　　edifice—
Received the outraged corpse with a spiritual kiss;
Consigned the last remains of the Actor to the grave
With a prayer that God would claim him from Jordan's
　　mystic wave.
　　Thus may honor ever bind thee, both happy one and
　　　mourner,
In bonds of love and union to that " Church Around the
　　Corner."

5

War;

OR, PRESENT AND FUTURE.

—o—

XUBERANT beauties hail the dawn of day,
 The vesture of the earth is fair and gay,
 Sweet flowers unfold their tinted leaves to view,
 And greet the sunlight and the glist'ning dew.
Dense forests in communion whisper words
Of welcome; and bright plumaged, joyous birds
Thrill with melodious notes the vaulted sky,
While soaring larks, lost to the human eye,
Enrapt the ear and fascinate the soul
With melting streams of melody, which roll
Thro' empty space, as 'twere an angel's voice,
Bidding all living nature to rejoice.
 Fair children sport, in happy, thoughtless groups,
Existing but in present joy and hopes.
The mother, in the fulness of her love,
Maternal pride and joy, lives but to prove
Her heart's devotion to her child and spouse,
And make each day, from dawn until its close,

A cradled happiness, to glad each heart,
And to each nature generous joys impart.
All sympathetic nature, every phase
Of life is tinted by the beauteous rays
Which gild the hour of peace. But now, alas!
A change comes o'er the scene, and whispers pass
From ear to ear, of ominous import,
And soon there spreads the terrible " report "
That joy must flee, and fondest hopes must yield
Their dearest treasure to the blood stained field;
That hearts must bleed, and bosoms rend with woe,
While dear ones fall in death, before the foe!
For, some affront to arrogance and power
Bids thousands die within a passing hour,
And wash away the stain with streams of blood,
While he who spills it, in a sullen mood,
Looks on with callous eye and deadened care
For all the crimes his evil work may bear.
Fair lands are trampled 'neath the warrior's steed,
And grandest beauties claim no moment's heed;
Famine and pestilence grow swiftly rife,
Crushing to death the noblest, strongest life.
    Grand structures, monuments of ancient skill,
Are dealt destruction by the imperious will
Of one great tyrant; while all nations wait,
In stern, grim silence, the award of *Fate.*
    While nations reign, and power sustains its sway,
War will ne'er cease to cloud the sunniest day,
And carnivals of blood will madly urge
Their myriad vot'ries to the awful verge

Of agony and death, from age to age,
'Till death shall silence every warrior's rage;
For, while evil lurks in human breast,
'Twill ever strive, with vengeful ire, to wrest
Each gift which Nature portions to the just,
And seek to sacrifice its dearest trust;
Unscrupulous, ambitious aims will force
Life's purest current from its peaceful course;
And, were no hand upraised to intercept,
Progress and civilization would be swept,
By one relentless tyrant's vengeful breath,
In the oblivion of moral death.
So wars must wage, and warriors must arm
To save an honored name and right from harm,
And check the hordes which would imbue their hands
In despoilation of the fairest lands.

Thus FRANCE, whose conq'ring hosts besciged the
And e'er victorious, mightest despots hurled　　[world,
From pinnacles of power to depths of shame,
Humiliation, and of blasted fame,
Now subjugated lies beneath the heel
Of one she rashly deemed would meekly kneel.
And render each concession on demand,
Or else would fall beneath her upraised hand.
For years her ships have spread the ocean's wave,
And challenged foes her mighty strength to brave;
Her frowning forts were deemed impregnable
To heaviest guns and storms of seething shell;
Her mighty armies nations held in awe,
Who, in her vaunted greatness, victory saw

But years of peace wro't revelry and ease,
And Paris reigned for nought except to please
Voluptuous sense; Science and Art imposed
A tribute from all lands, and Fashion posed
The ingenuity of all the earth
To wrest her from the land which gave her birth;
But the great vigor and majestic power
Of martial strength waned with each fleeting hour,
And when Napoleon arrogantly sought
T' renew the task his predecessor taught,
And forced the German vet'rans in the field
To combat for the rights they scorned to yield,
His armies fled before the powerful arm
O'er which great Justice held a with'ring charm.
The Emperor, at Sedan, resigned his sword,
And there the Empire fell, to be restored
Refined and purged—but as an Empire reign
Until *legitimately* it shall resign
Its ancient honors, titles, name and fame—
That grand Republic *principle* shall claim
Its children as its lawful wards—till truth
Shall dawn upon its free, unshackled youth.

Thus "Imperial France" has fallen at last,
And all its pride and arrogance is past.
The retribution due unholy deeds
Sternly confronts her while she cruelly bleeds.
"Invulnerable Paris," doomed by Fate
To German legions to capitulate,
Must lay her majesty upon the dust,
And bow her head, and eat the bitter crust.

But may she *rise* and profit by the past,
For, tho' an Empire still, she's nearing fast
The day when Freedom shall ascend its throne
And claim her wand'ring children as its own..

But years must pass ere evils long instilled
In corrupt soil, howe'er it may be tilled,
Shall *yield* its tares, and full eared wheat replace
The rank weeds fostered by a former race.
Aye! Years must pass, and generations die,
And mighty Truth *long* battle with a lie
Ere *Liberty* proclaims that kings have lain
Their sceptres down, and the firm soldered chain
Which binds the human race as slaves to power
Shall burst its bonds, and Freedom claim its dower.
Then " *La Grande Nation* " shall receive its choice
Without a murmur or dissenting voice—
Its noble people weave a glorious thread,
Which, borne on Freedom's wings, shall swiftly spread
O'er land and sea, until it shall unite,
In everlasting bonds of might and right,
With the REPUBLIC of our RANSOMED STATES,
And open to the *world* its long closed gates.

To My Friends.

—o—

FRIENDSHIP we cry—the echo's mocking sound
Replies thro' empty space—unknown—unfound!
How strict our search our labor may be lost,
Except experience outset the cost;
But 'neath a bed of dross the jewel lies,
Hid from the searching glance of many eyes,
Diffusing purest germs of beauteous life—
An antidote to all its care and strife—
E'en as the violet, on its mossy bank,
Diffuses sweetness from a bed so rank
That it might bloom unseen, and fade, and die,
Did not its perfume point to where it lie,
And, 'mid the vacillating hues which blend
And tarnish the pure rays which angels lend
To deck the name of FRIEND, unnumbered beams
Have crossed my checkered path as fitful dreams,
And when reality was most intense
The vision fled and left but vapid sense;
But still some friends have stood each fiery test,
And pass'd unscathed what scattered all the rest.

And ye who've proved yourselves my firm and true
Unswerving friends, accept your simple due,
My grateful thanks, and earnest blessing on
The many cherished kindness', ye have done—
And when the sun of mortal life shall wane,
And heaven claim its precious gift again,
May eternal bonds unite our souls in love
In the bright home of bliss prepared above.

www.ingramcontent.com/pod-product-compliance
Lightning Source LLC
Chambersburg PA
CBHW020808020726
47495CB00008B/2640